Contents

Unit 1	Hello	2
Unit 2	Family	9
Review 1		16
Unit 3	Classroom	17
Unit 4	Toys	24
Review 2		31
Unit 5	Animals	33
Unit 6	Food	40
Review 3		47
Unit 7	Clothes	49
Unit 8	Home	56
Review 4		63

MACMILLAN

Jeanne Perrett

Unit 1 Lesson 1 — Hello

1

2  a

a

1 Listen. Sing.
2 Listen and repeat. Trace and colour.

1 Lesson 2

1 Listen and repeat. Trace and colour.

value I say hello to my friends.

1 Lesson 3

1

4

1   **2**

1 Listen and sing.
2 Listen and repeat. Trace and colour. Sing.

1 Lesson 4

1 Listen. Act it out.

1 Lesson 5

2

1 Sing and play.
2 Listen and repeat. Trace and colour. Sing.

Lesson 6
Big Wide World

1 Listen. Circle.

Lesson 7

1 Find and colour.

Unit 2 — Family
Lesson 1

1

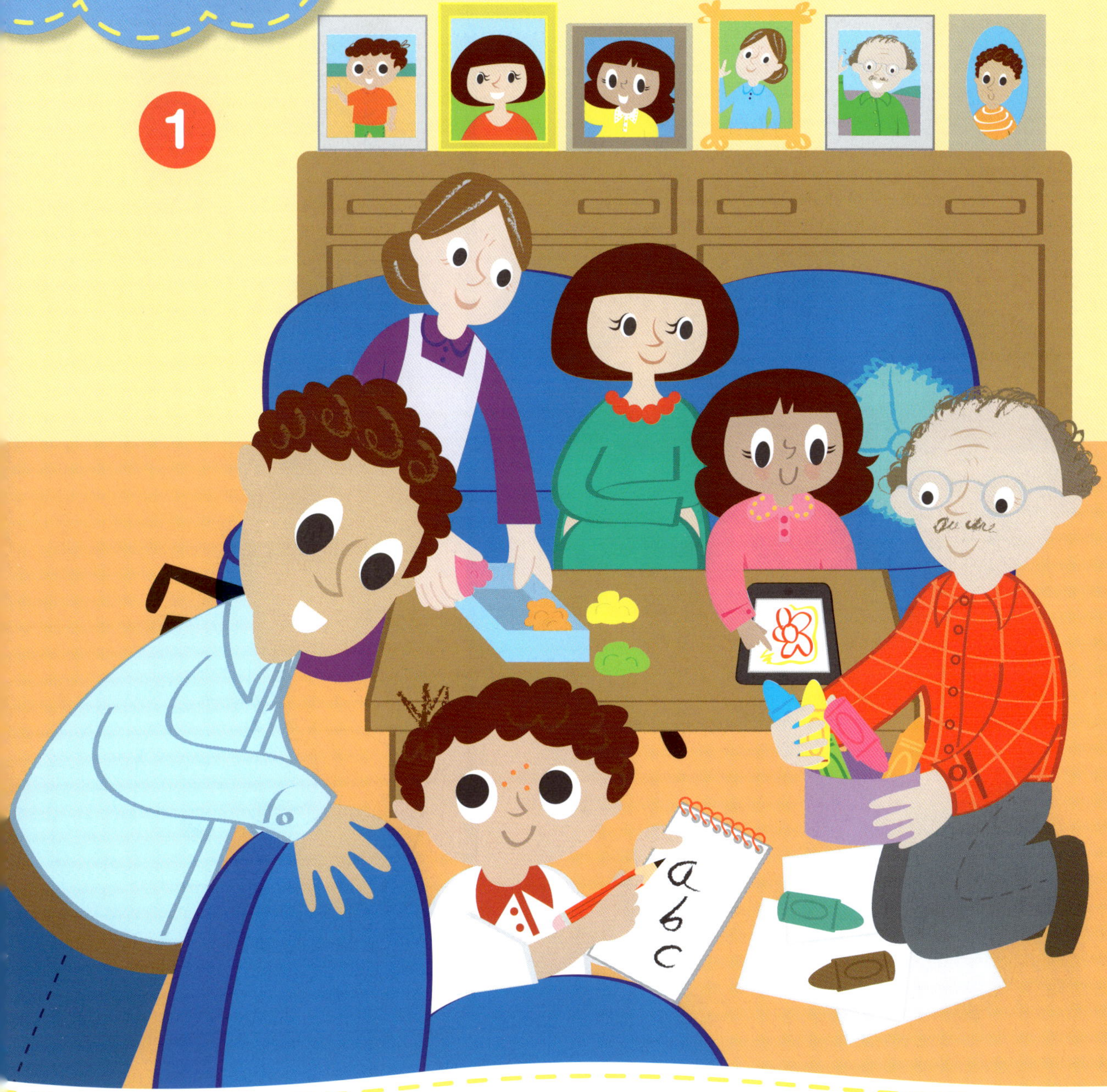

2

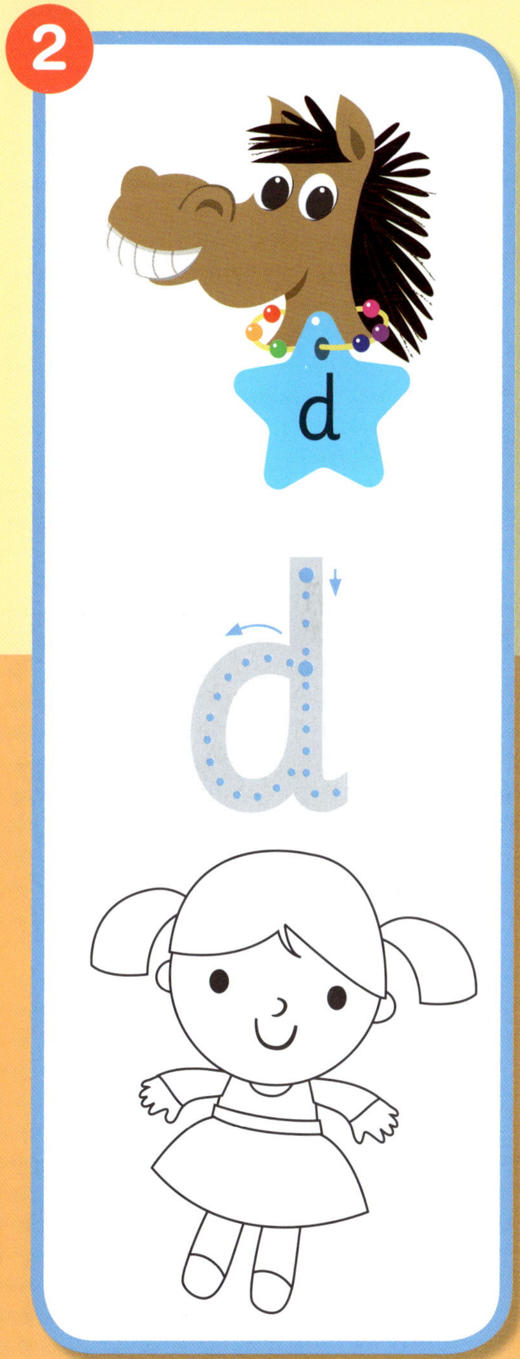

1 Listen and repeat. Sing.
2 Listen and repeat. Trace and colour.

 I'm tidy.

2 Lesson 2

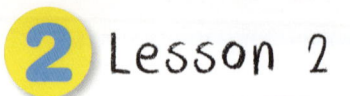

1 Sing. Match.
2 Listen and repeat. Trace and colour.

② Lesson 3

①

②

①   ②

1 Match and say.
2 Listen and repeat. Trace and colour. Sing.

2 Lesson 4

1 Listen. Act it out.

2 Lesson 5

1 Match.
2 Listen and repeat. Trace and colour. Sing.

2 Lesson 6 — Big Wide World

1

1 Find and circle.

② Lesson 7

①

②

 ①  ②

1 Make and play.
2 Listen and repeat. Colour. Sing.

15

Review 1

1

1 Point and say. Listen and colour.

Unit 3
Lesson 1

Classroom

1

2

g

g

  **1**   1 Listen and repeat. Sing.
2 Listen and repeat. Trace and colour.

 I'm not too noisy.

17

3 Lesson 2

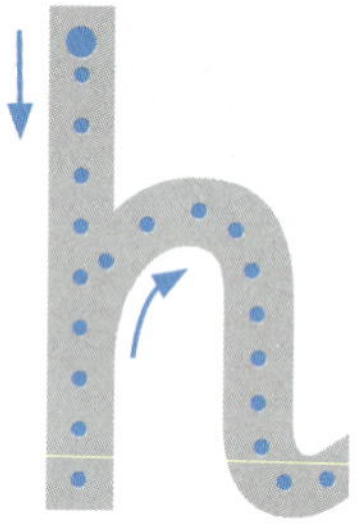

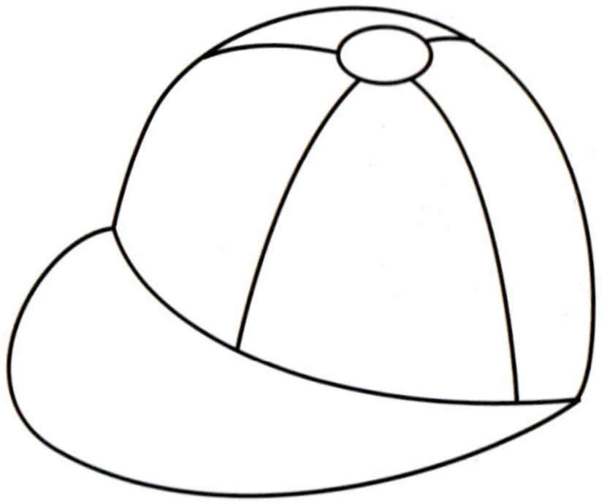

1

2

18

1 Sing. Match.
2 Listen and repeat. Trace and colour.

3 Lesson 3

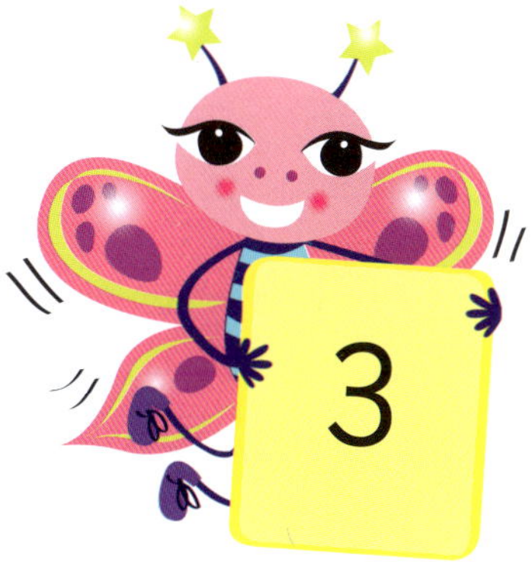

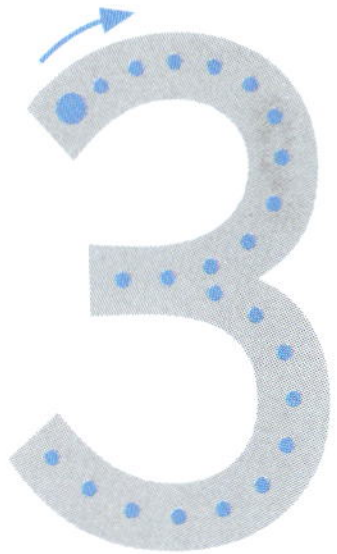

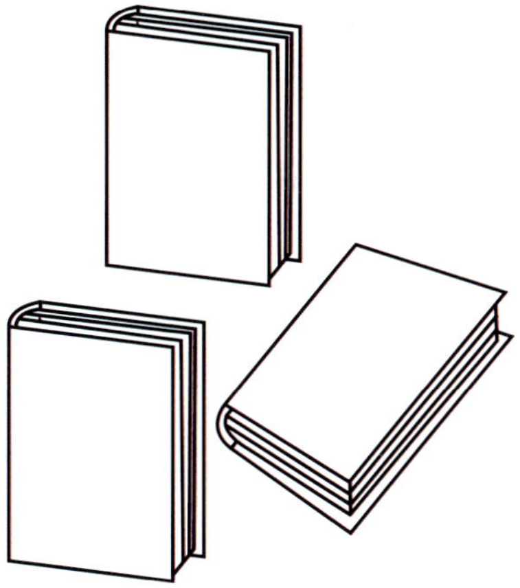

1 Circle.
2 Listen and repeat. Trace and colour. Sing.

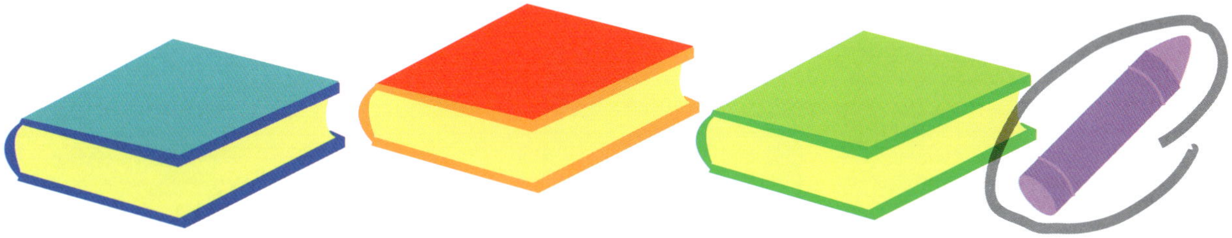

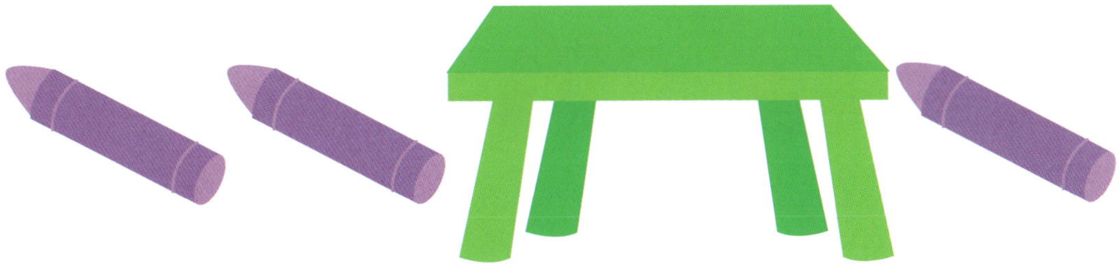

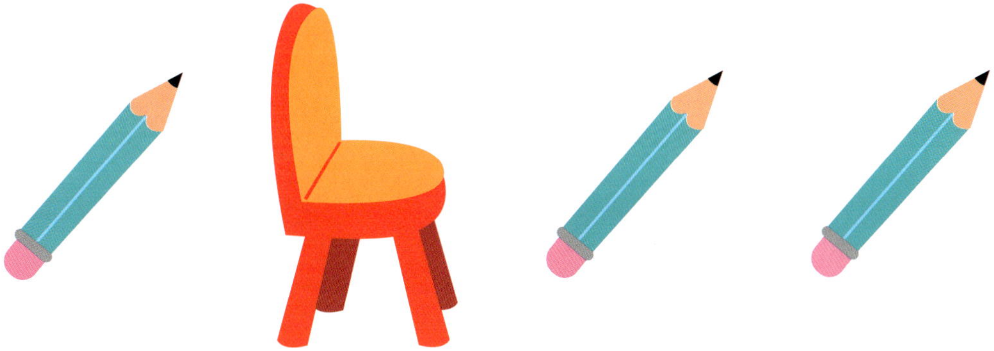

3 Lesson 4

1 Listen. Act it out.

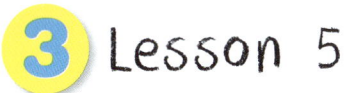 Lesson 5

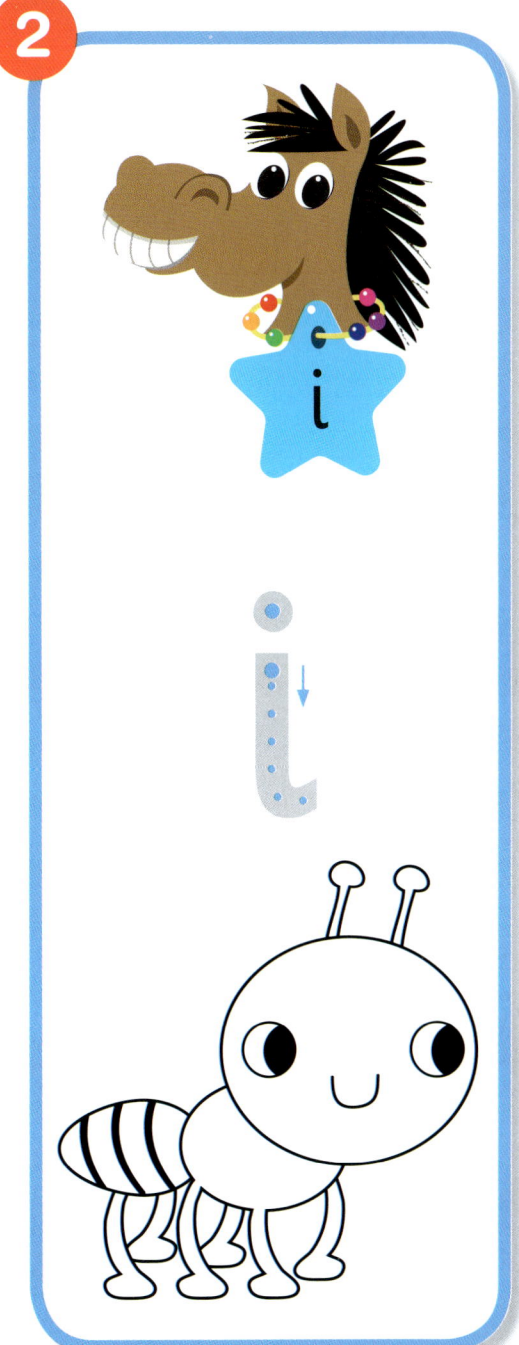

1 Listen. Play and say.
2 Listen and repeat. Trace and colour. Sing

3 Lesson 6 — Big Wide World

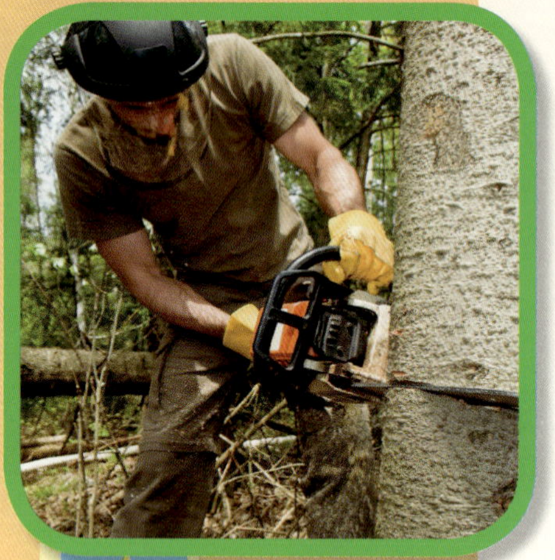

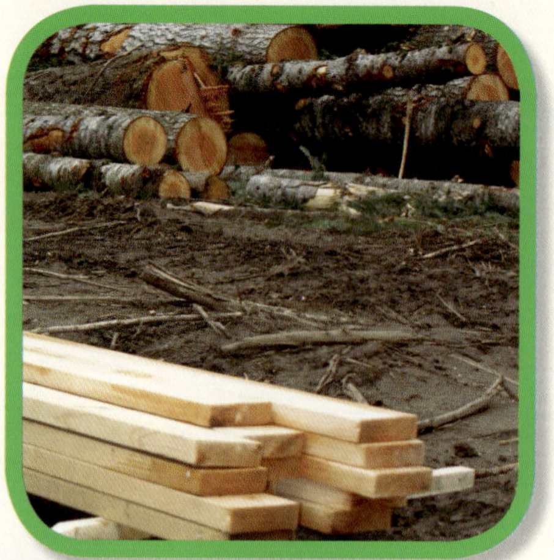

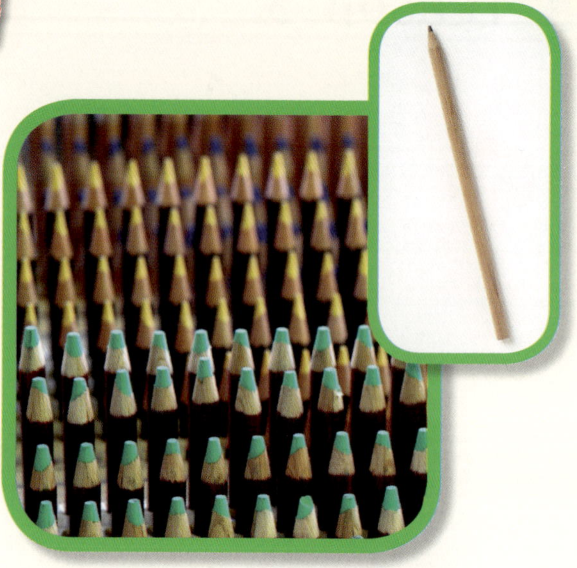

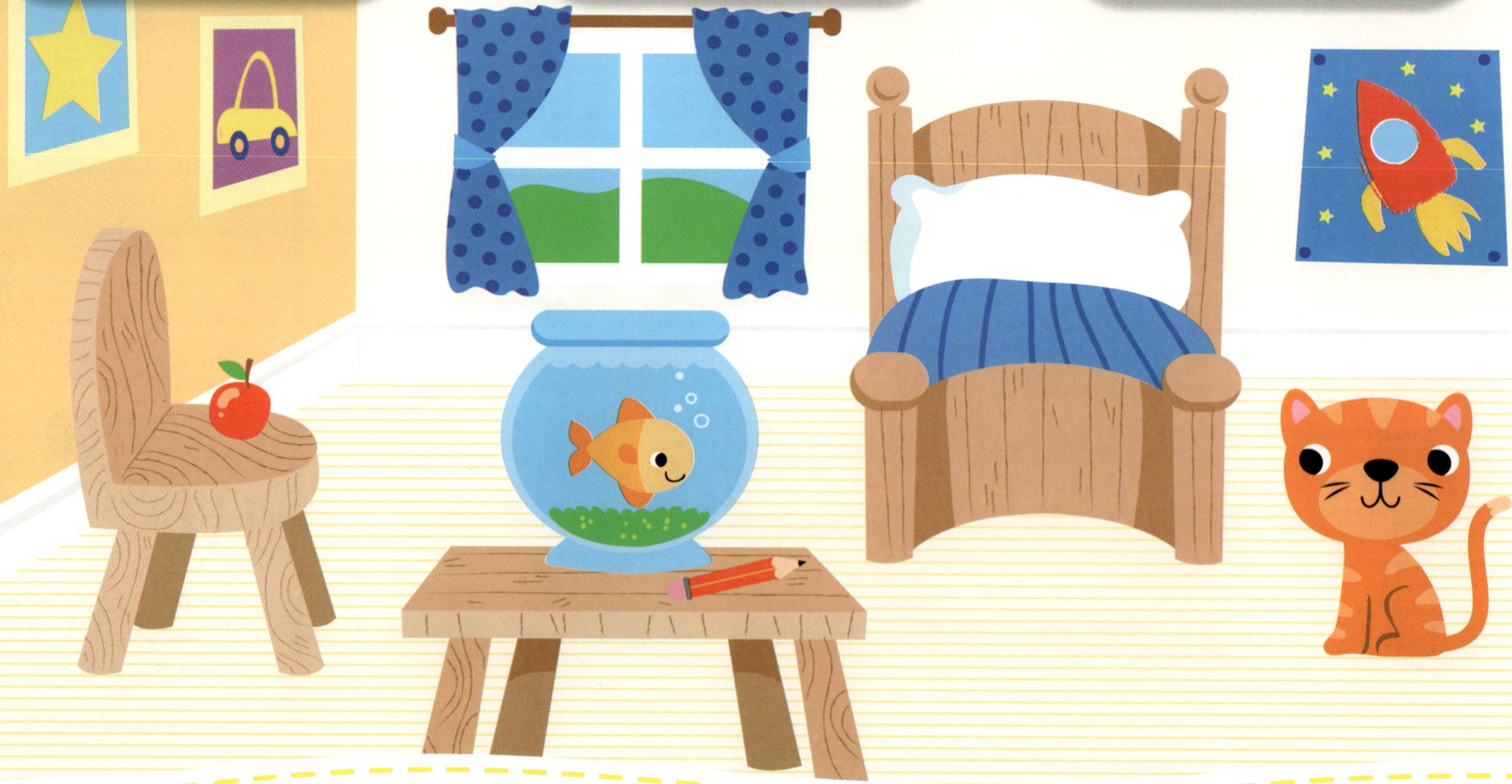

1

1 Circle.

3 Lesson 7

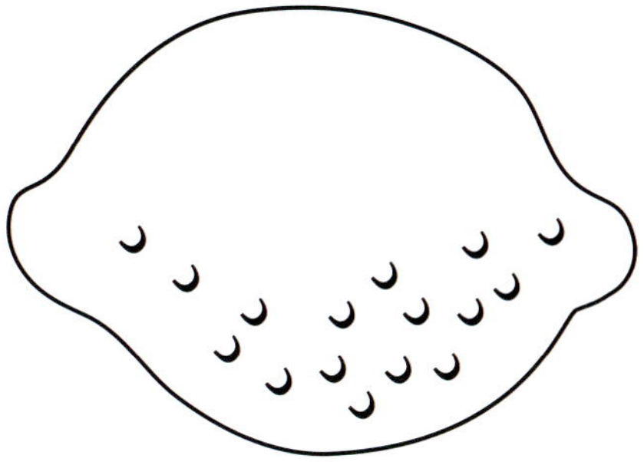

1

2

1 Colour.
2 Listen and repeat. Colour. Sing.

23

Unit 4 Lesson 1 — Toys

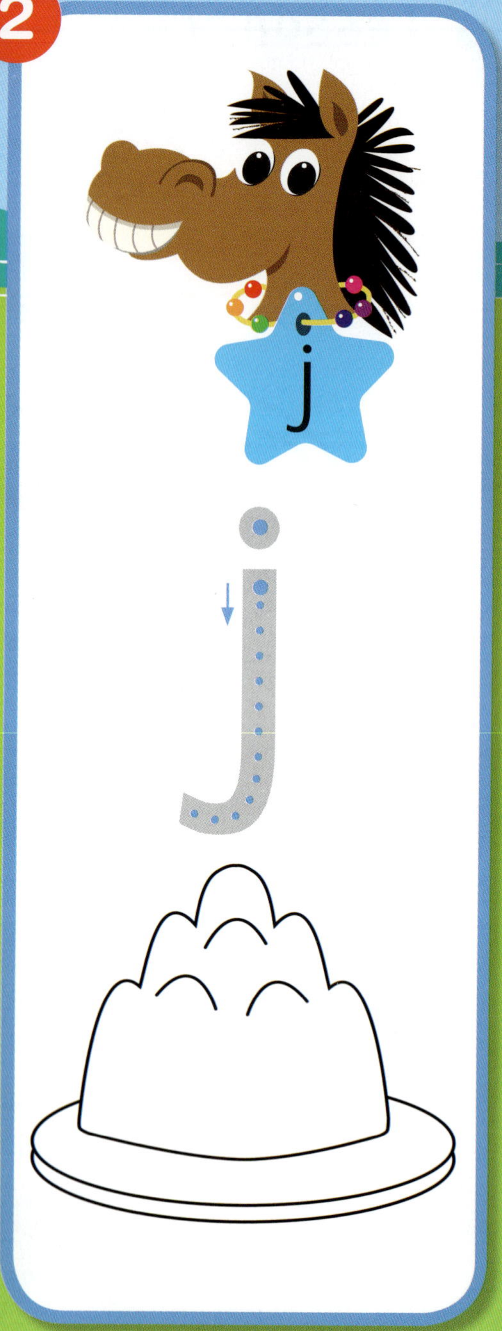

1 Listen and repeat. Sing.
2 Listen and repeat. Trace and colour.

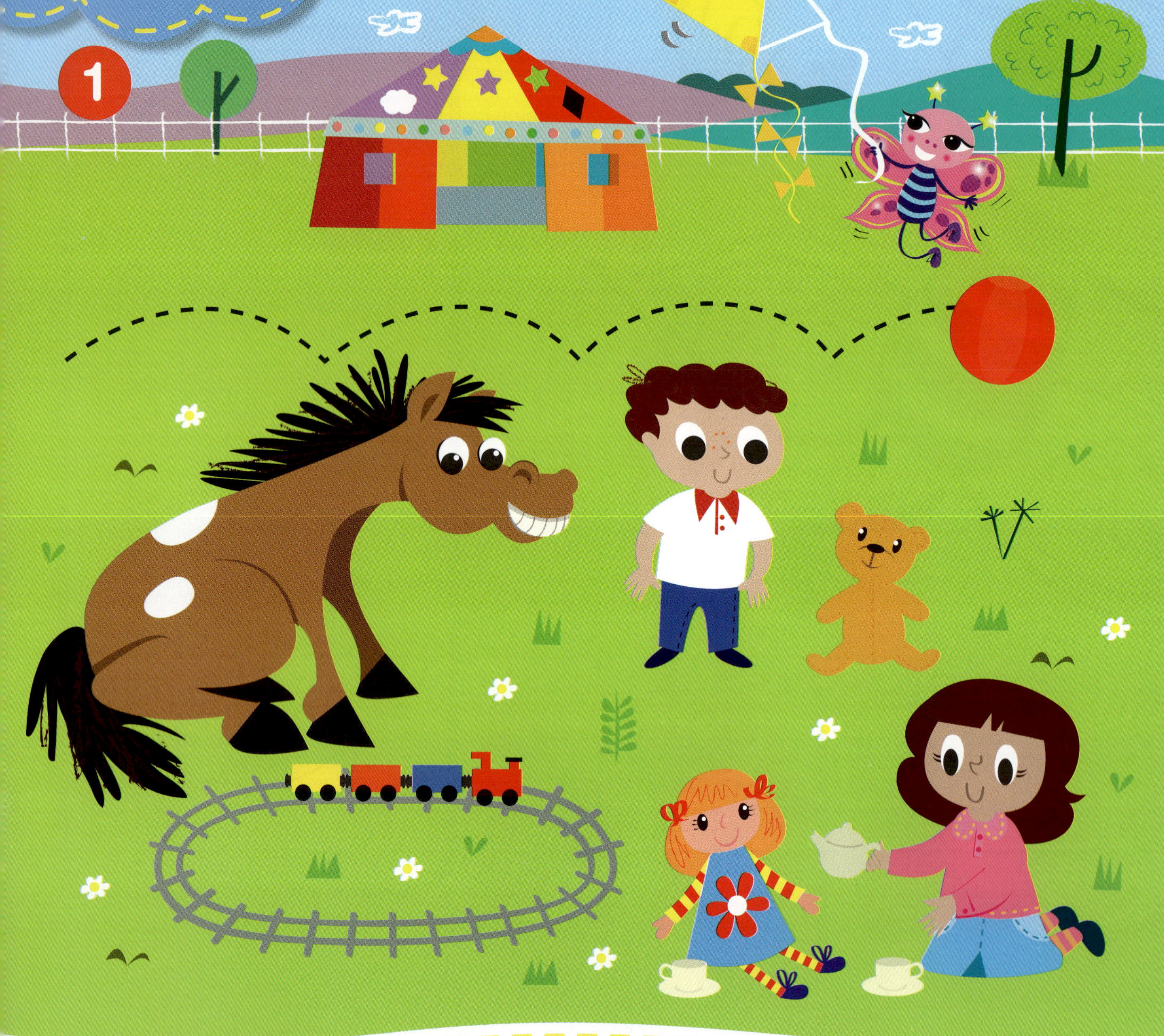

I put rubbish in the bin.

4 Lesson 2

1

2

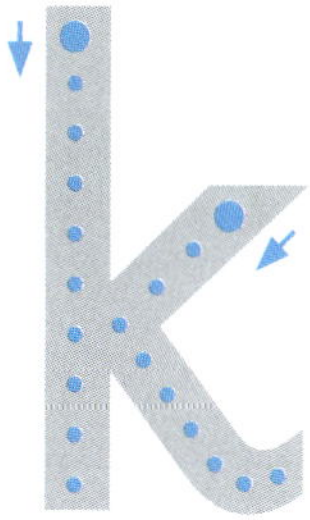

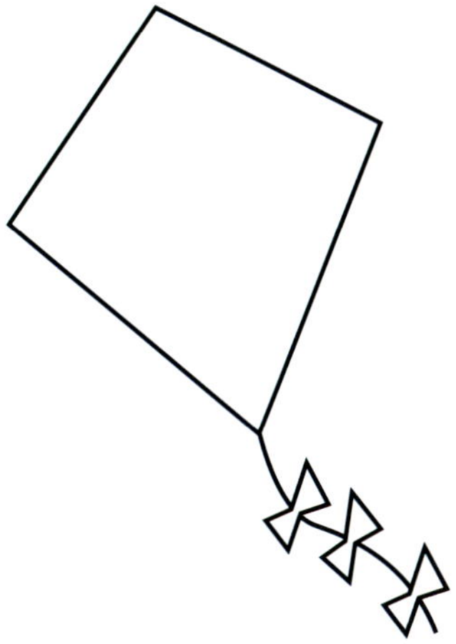

1 Circle. Sing.
2 Listen and repeat. Trace and colour.

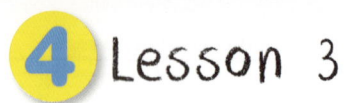

Lesson 3

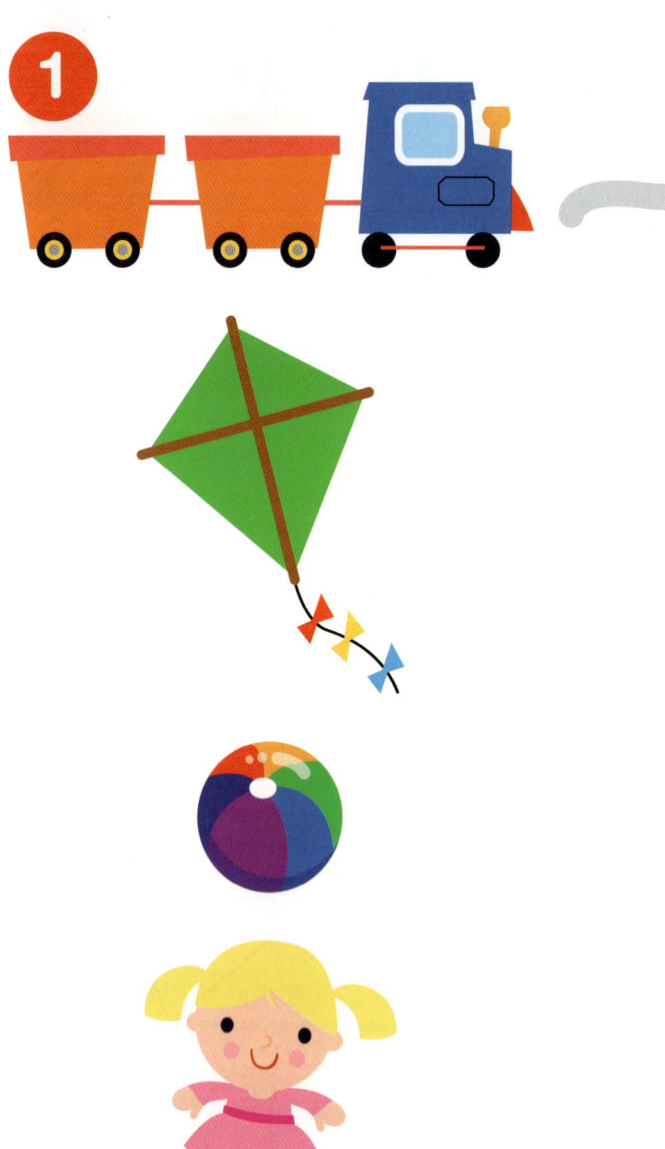

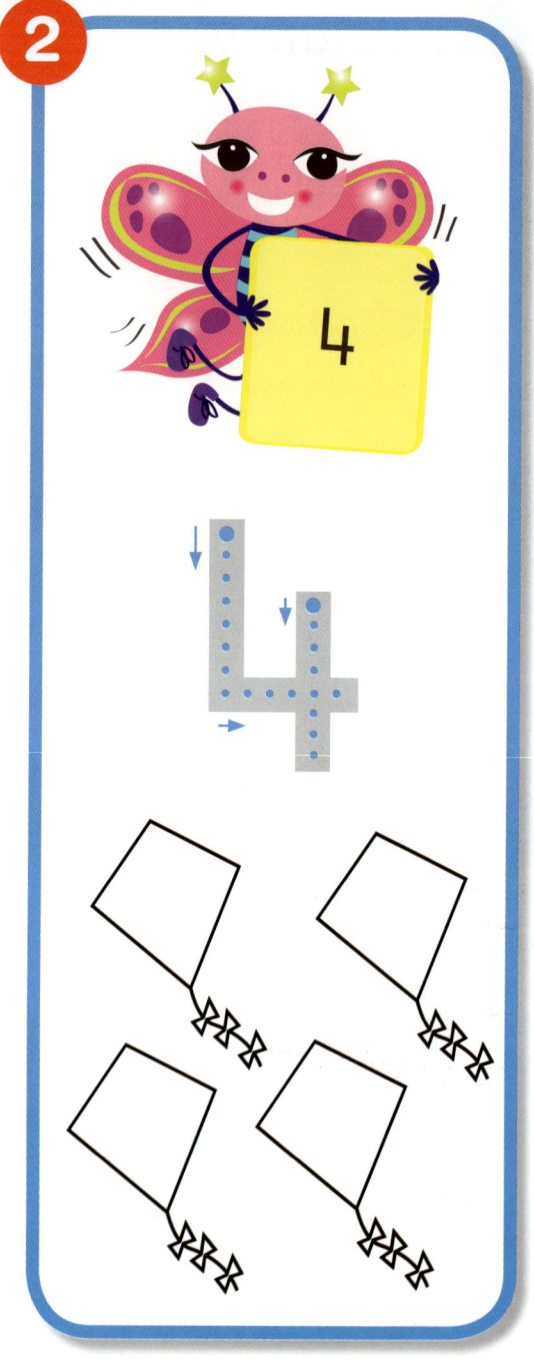

1 Match.
2 Listen and repeat. Trace and colour. Sing.

4 Lesson 4

1 Listen. Act it out.

4 Lesson 5

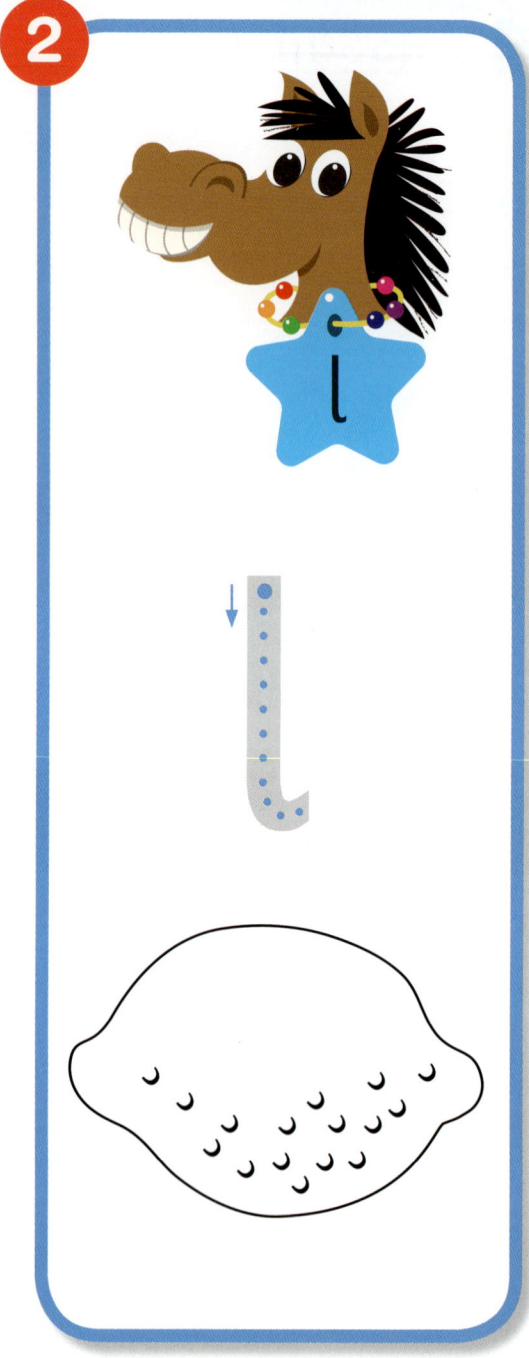

1. Play and say.
2. Listen and repeat. Trace and colour. Sing.

4 Lesson 6 — Big Wide World

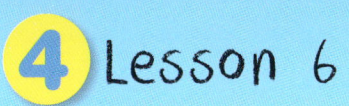

1 Colour.

4 Lesson 7

1

2

1 Match.
2 Listen and repeat. Colour. Sing.

Review 2

1

1 Point and say. Listen and colour.

31

Review 2

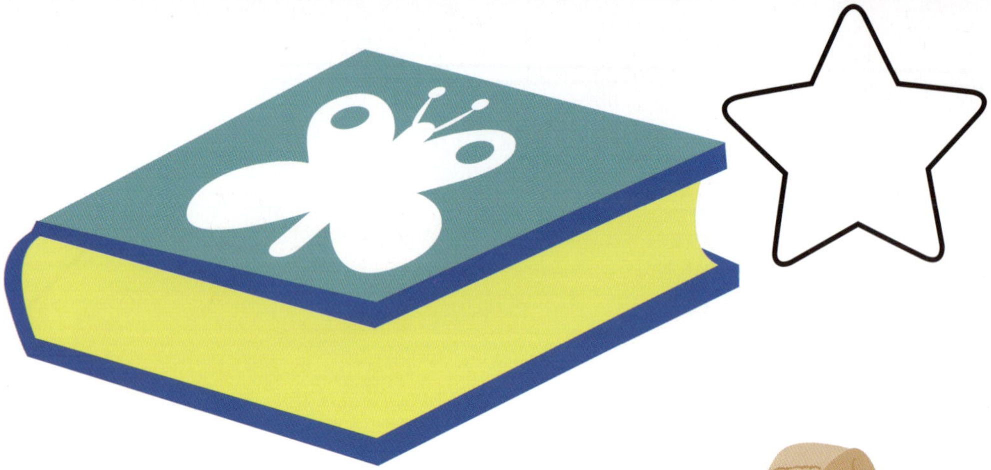

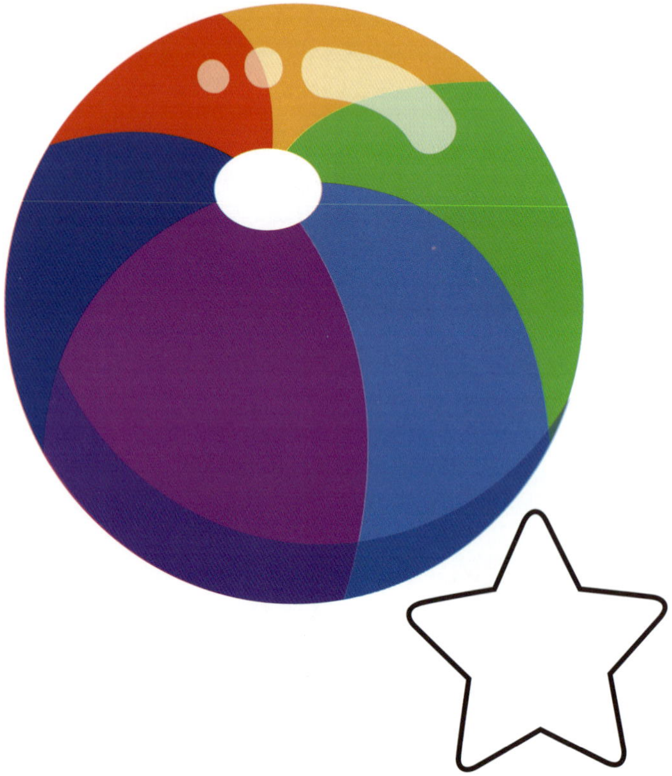

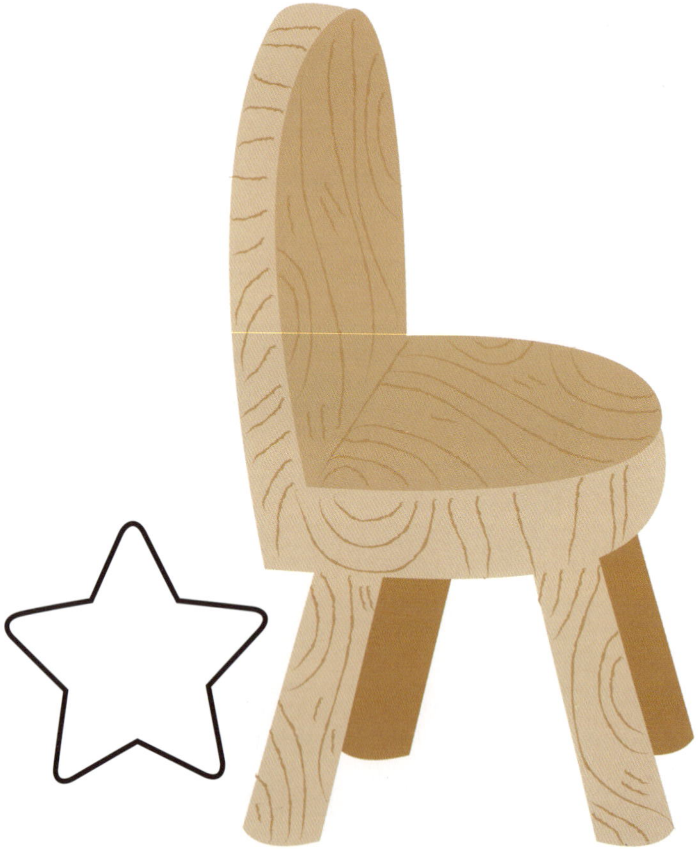

1

1 Point and say. Listen and colour.

Unit 5 — Animals

Lesson 1

m

    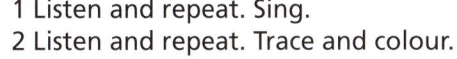 

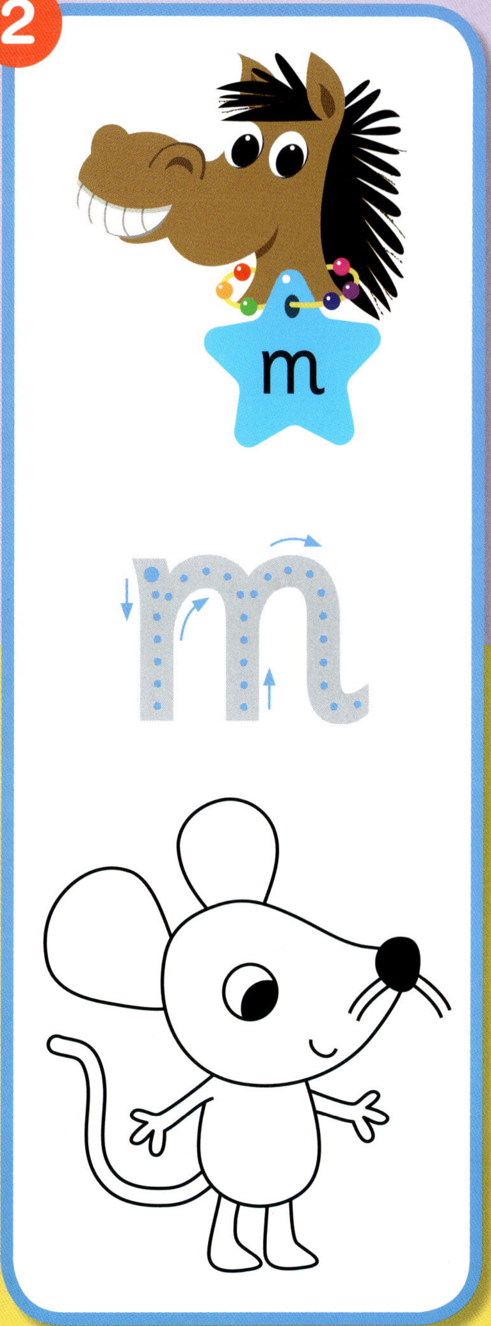

1 Listen and repeat. Sing.
2 Listen and repeat. Trace and colour.

value: I'm kind to animals.

33

5 Lesson 2

34

1 Match. Sing.
2 Listen and repeat. Trace and colour.

5 Lesson 3

1

2

1 2

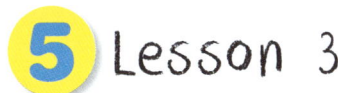

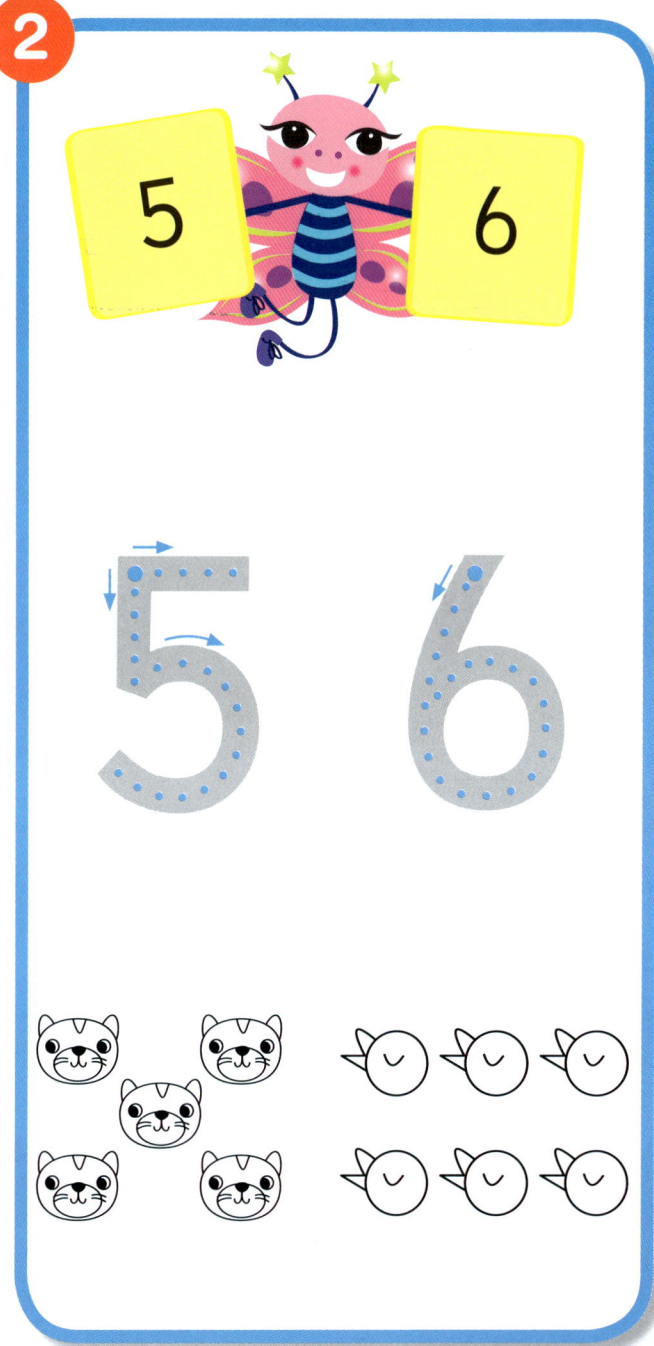

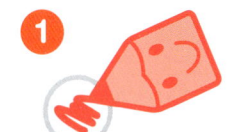

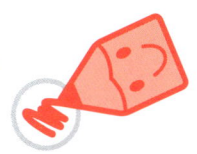

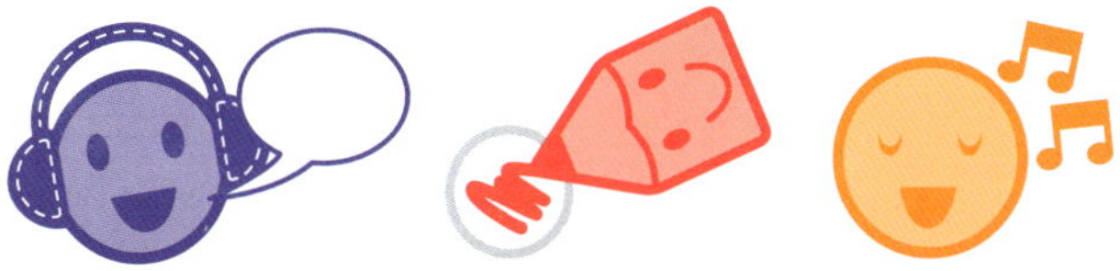

1 Colour.
2 Listen and repeat. Trace and colour. Sing.

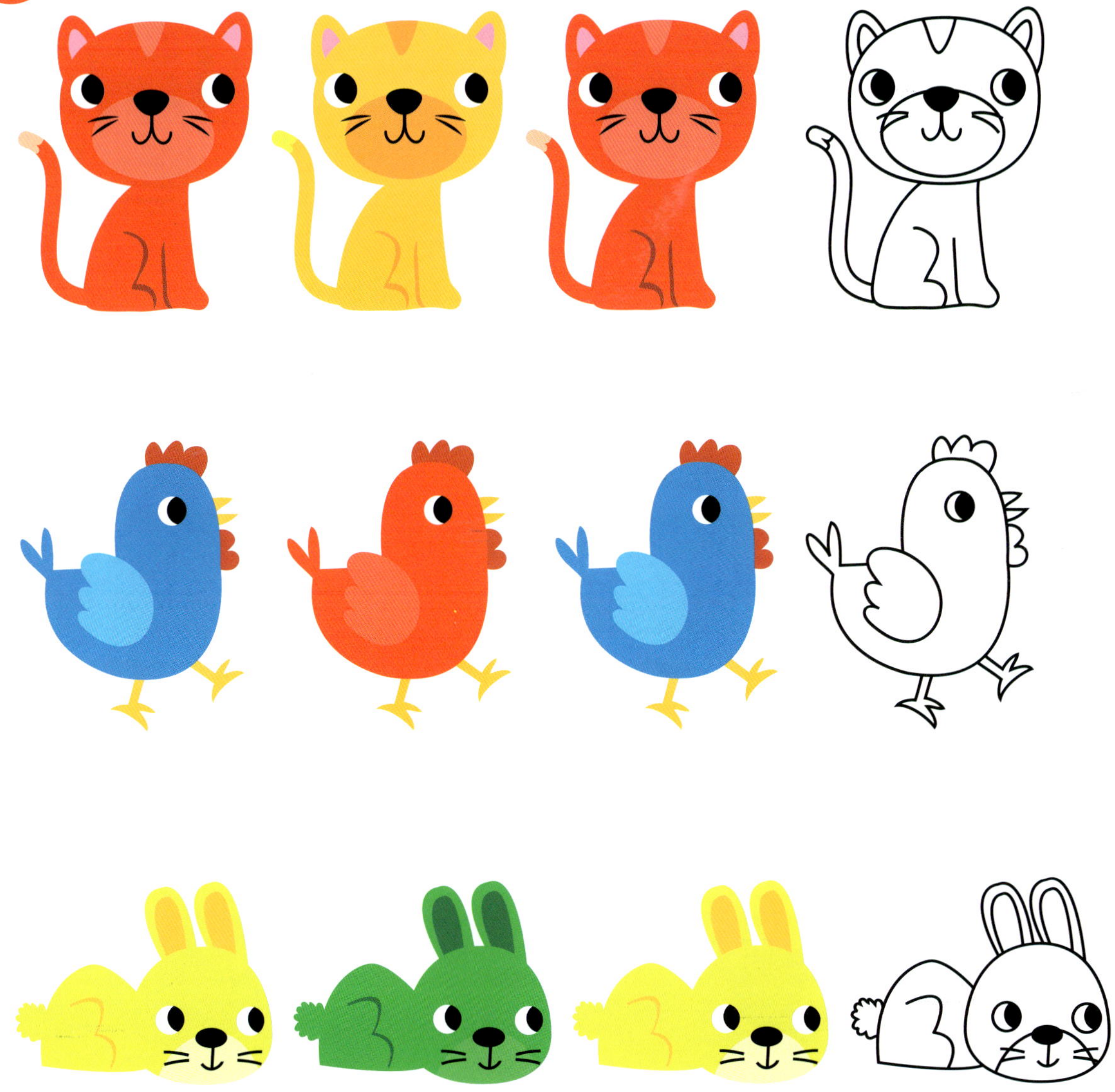

5 Lesson 4

1 Listen. Act it out.

Lesson 5

o p

1 Match.
2 Listen and repeat. Trace and colour. Sing.

5 Lesson 6 — Big Wide World

1

1 Match.

38

5 Lesson 7

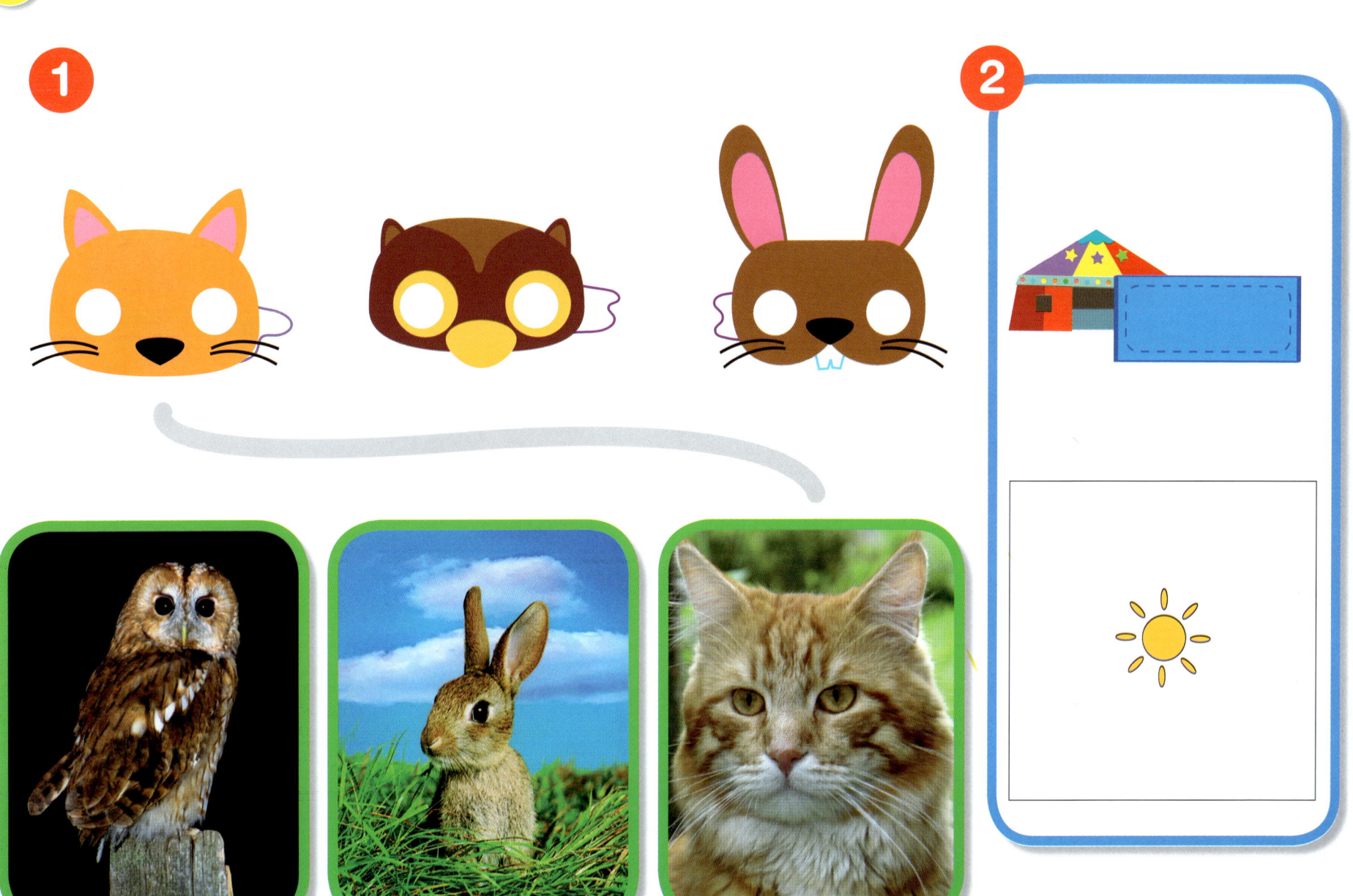

1

2

1 Match.
2 Listen and repeat. Colour. Sing.

Unit 6
Lesson 1

Food

1

2

q

q

40

1 Listen and repeat. Sing.
2 Listen and repeat. Trace and colour.

6 Lesson 2

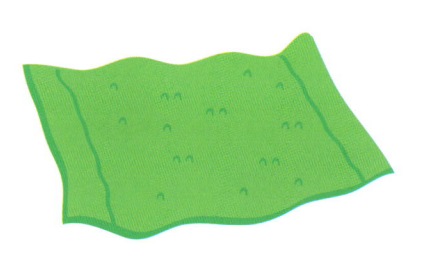

2
r

r

1 Match. Sing.
2 Listen and repeat. Trace and colour.

value — I wash my hands.

41

6 Lesson 3

1

2

7 8

42

1 Listen and circle.
2 Listen and repeat. Trace and colour. Sing.

6 Lesson 4

1 Listen. Act it out

43

6 Lesson 5

1

2

s t

44

1 Match.
2 Listen and repeat. Trace and colour. Sing.

6 Lesson 6 — Big Wide World

1 Colour.

45

6 Lesson 7

1 Make.
2 Match. Colour.
3 Listen and repeat. Colour. Sing.

46

Review 3

1

1 Point and say. Listen and colour.

47

Review 3

1

1 Point and say. Listen and colour.

Unit 7 Lesson 1

Clothes

1
2

u
u

1 Listen and repeat. Sing.
2 Listen and repeat. Trace and colour.

49

7 Lesson 2

1

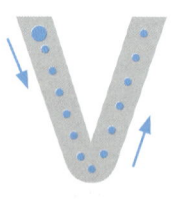

2

50

1 Match. Sing.
2 Listen and repeat. Trace and colour.

value — I take my shoes off in the house.

7 Lesson 3

1

2

1 Circle.
2 Listen and repeat. Trace and colour. Sing.

7 Lesson 4

1 Listen. Act it out.

52

Lesson 5

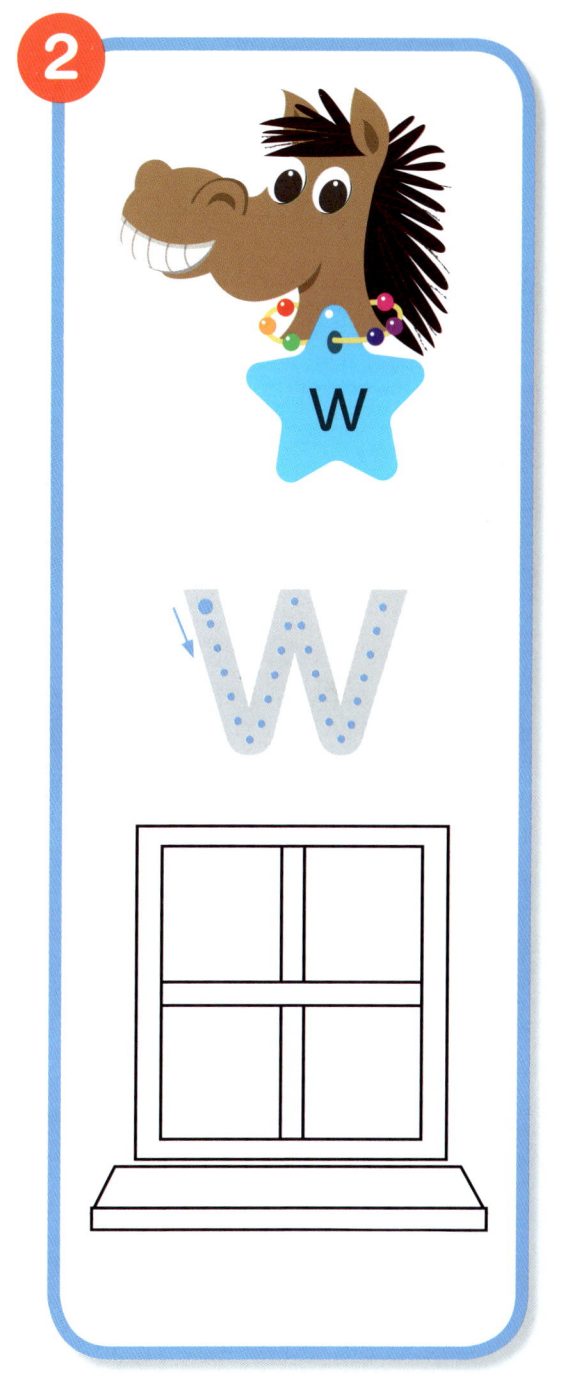

1

2

1 Match.
2 Listen and repeat. Trace and colour. Sing.

53

7 Lesson 6 — Big Wide World

1 Colour.

7 Lesson 7

1     
2

1 Match.
2 Listen and repeat. Colour. Sing.

55

Unit 8 — Lesson 1

Home

a b c d e f g h i j k l

1 Listen and repeat. Point and say. Sing.

8 Lesson 2

1

n o p q r s t u v w x y z

1 Listen and find.

Value I like my home.

57

8 Lesson 3

2

10

58

1 Match.
2 Listen and repeat. Trace and colour. Sing.

8 Lesson 4

1 Listen. Act it out.

59

8 Lesson 5

1

2

x y z

60

Lesson 6 — Big Wide World

1 Point and say. Colour.

8 Lesson 7

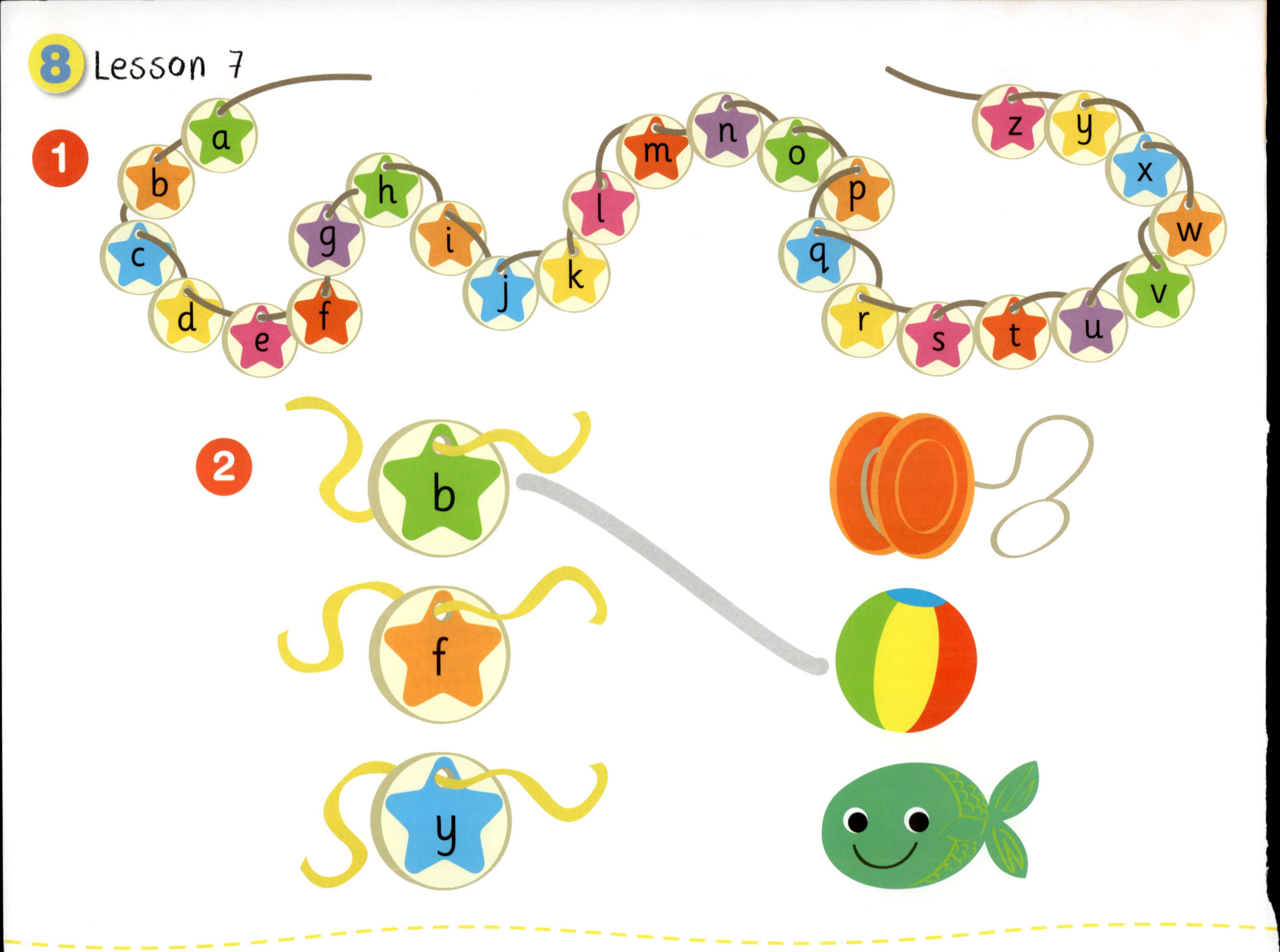

1

a b c d e f g h i j k l m n o p q r s t u v w x y z

2

1 Make.
2 Match.

Review 4

1

1 Point and say. Listen and colour.

63

Review 4

1

1 Point and say. Listen and colour.